from
CONSCIOUSNESS
to
CONSCIOUSNESS

Other books by Ramesh S. Balsekar:

* *A Duet Of One*
* *The Final Truth*
* *Experiencing The Teaching*
* *Explorations Into The Eternal*
* *Experience Of Immortality*
* *Pointers From Nisargadatta Maharaj*

from
CONSCIOUSNESS
to
CONSCIOUSNESS

Letters of
Ramesh S. Balsekar
December 1987 - July 1988

ADVAITA PRESS
-LOS ANGELES-

Second Edition: 1989

Previously published as *From Conciousness To Conciousness*

All rights reserved. No part of this book may be reproduced or transmitted in any form or by any means, electronic or mechanical, including photocopying, recording, or by any information storage and retreival system without written permission from the author or his agents, except for the inclusion of brief quotations in a review.

Copyright © 1989 by

Ramesh S. Balsekar

First Published in United States Of America by

ADVAITA PRESS

P.O. Box 3479

Redondo Beach, California 90277

Designed by: Wayne Liquorman

Cover Design: Christopher Johnson

Library of Congress Catalog Card Number: 89-84768

ISBN 0-929448-10-3   10 9 8 7 6 5 4 3 2 1

**ALL THERE IS
IS CONSCIOUSNESS**

EDITOR'S NOTE

The following letters, which were written by Ramesh to me and another disciple, are not only exquisite presentations of his teaching as such, but they also embody a beautiful demonstration of an extremely important, but very subtle aspect of his teaching, which is the *guru*-disciple relationship. The very writing of the letters is a form of Love communion between *guru* and disciple (as Love is defined by Ramesh on p. 61). In essence, the relationship from the perspective of the *guru* is an impersonal one, as Ramesh reports in the case of his own *guru*: "Maharaj repeatedly asserts that his words are not addressed to any individual entity but to Consciousness. Words arise from Consciousness and are addressed to Consciousness."[1]

Since a letter is apparently addressed to an individual, there appears to be a paradox here. To the *guru*, however, there is no contradiction since he sees the recipient of the letter as Consciousness and not "other" than himself. And when letters of a *guru* are published (in the case of a *jnani*, an exceedingly rare, if not unique circumstance), precisely because they are letters there is in them a certain charm associated with the warmth of intimacy which could hardly be expected to occur in more formal works written specifically for publication.

---

1. Ramesh S. Balsekar, *Pointers From Nisargadatta Maharaj* (Bombay: Chetana, 1982), p.190 (subsequently referred to as *Pointers*)

And so, in addition to giving us details about the closeness of his relationship with his own *guru*, and also telling us in his eloquent style stories (which are not only interesting and informative, but downright entertaining) about his relationship with his disciples, he can be seen relating patiently and compassionately to the needs of his correspondents.

There is obviously no way that a disciple can reciprocate the gift he receives from his *guru*. Nevertheless, the profound feelings of gratitude can engender powerful motivations "to do something". It occurred to me that I might return the words through which Ramesh's gift was given to me. I assembled all the letters I had received from Ramesh, edited them, typed them, and had them reproduced in the form of an 85-page booklet to be presented to him upon his return to the United States this year.

Only five copies were made. There was no intention of having the booklet published. Ramesh saw otherwise. As *guru*, his words were not addressed to an individual but to Consciousness, which we all are. He saw that the booklet might well serve both disciples and non-disciples.

With the exception of a very few minor changes and the addition of this note, the publication is essentially identical in form and content to the unpublished version. Perhaps one editorial decision that was carried over from the original should be mentioned. Although Ramesh tells us about a considerable number of his disciples, and directly addresses two of them, none have been identified by name. Indeed, aside from those of a few public personalities who are cited only in reference to something that has been published by or about them, the only names given in the text are those of Nisargadatta Maharaj and Ramana Maharshi.

Now you, the reader of this, are being offered the inexpressible gift of Ramesh. As he says: "The grace of the *guru* is like an ocean - it is entirely up to the disciple how much of the ocean he wants and how much he can carry! And even this is only a concept. Truly there is no duality of *guru* and disciple, and this realization brings the search to an end"[2].

October 1988

---

2. Ramesh S. Balsekar, *Explorations Into The Eternal* (Bombay: Chetana, 1987), p.4 (subsequently referred to as *Explorations*)

December 22, 1987

From the moment I first met you, I knew you were one of those rare, sincere seekers. I saw it in your eyes. You didn't say a word -- you merely extended your hand to offer me a lovely orchid. And thereafter you brought a lovely orchid every time we met -- a sincere offering gratefully accepted.

And since then, I have watched your "progress". And *it* will arrive as soon as the "seeking" spontaneously drops off! There is nothing "you" can do about it -- and that is at once the inherent contradiction: a sense of frustration together with a sense of tremendous relief!

January 18, 1988

Relatively speaking, there is no "reason" to think that I prefer one person to another because there is something extremely natural and spontaneous which brings about an affinity between persons. The only way to look at it is that such natural affinity is obviously a part of the functioning of Totality -- and nothing in such functioning is without purpose, although such purpose may not be clear to the human mind (the split-mind).

Last week an American Swami came to see me. He joined the *ashram* in the U.S. 17 years ago, when he was 20. He was deeply interested in the subject of non-duality. It seems that at the *ashram*, more attention is given to the routine discipline than to the teaching and the practice, and he was therefore shaken to the core when he listened to what was given to me to say to him.

The fact that the totality of manifestation is merely an appearance in Consciousness and that its functioning is an *impersonal* and self-generated process in phenomenality, made a profound impression on him. He himself came to the spontaneous conclusion that therefore the individual human being, as the mere instrument through which this impersonal process occurs, cannot possibly have any autonomy or independence of volition and choice. He said he had waited more than 30 years for this authoritative confirmation of what he had "felt" since he was five years old! Nothing in this life is a coincidence. It was just a "chance" that had brought him to Bombay!

February 13, 1988

Regarding the instance of a *darshan* with F., when you suddenly realized that everything you did, "even down to body movements and facial expressions", had an egoic basis, it has to be necessarily so because the ego is the "operating centre" in the psychosomatic mechanism, operating through the brain: the brain is a part of the somatic mechanism while the operating centre in the driver's seat is a part of the psychic mechanism. And it is precisely for this reason that even a Ramana Maharshi or a Nisargadatta Maharaj will respond when called by name. In other words, the identification with the body-mind mechanism must continue so long as the body is alive and kicking! -- what enlightenment or understanding does is to remove the sense of doership which brought about the separation as an independent entity.

The basis of "true" understanding is truly simple: the totality of manifestation is an appearance in Consciousness, which arises precisely like the personal dream -- the waking dream and the personal dream are qualitatively not different in any way; its functioning is an *impersonal* and self-generated process in phenomenality, and it takes place through the billions of sentient beings as instruments.

An understanding of the impersonal nature of the functioning of Totality -- I am tempted to say, even an intellectual understanding -- brings about a curious phenomenon: not really the demolition of the ego, but the demolition (perhaps gradual) of the *fear of the ego*! Have I startled you?! It is a curious fact that the man who is thoroughly involved with life -- and its pleasures and miseries -- is not concerned with the ego. It is only when the mind happens to turn inward, and the "seeking" starts -- and the scriptures and the *gurus* have talked about the specter of the ego -- that the flight away from the ego begins; and the harder the running away from the ego, the stronger becomes the obsession with the ego. The whole of your letter describes this flight from the ego. And the horrible joke is that it is none other than the ego which is trying to run away from the ego!

The only way to deal with the ego is to understand what the ego is and how it has arisen: all there is is Consciousness, and it is the Consciousness which has *deliberately* identified itself with each individual body-mind mechanism in order to perceive the manifestation in the duality of observ*er*/observ*ed*. So, the entire functioning of the totality of manifestation -- the *lila* -- is an impersonal affair of evolution concerning the process of initial identification -- the identified existence covering a certain period -- the mind turning inward -- the beginning of the process of disidentification -- the progress of the disidentification -- and the final understanding of this very impersonal process, or enlightenment, in which Consciousness has regained its original "purity".

The understanding, as one Tao master has put it, is always sudden, but the deliverance may be gradual The deliverance is from the bondage of the *concept* of the ego; the gradual progress is the progress from the personal viewpoint into the impersonal perspective. The sudden understanding stops the flight from the ego, and this is what has happened in the case of the body-mind mechanism known relatively as O., and your entire letter traces the history of this flight to the point where the running away has ceased. What is now happening is witnessing which is not of the mind but of the impersonal noumenal. This is the "nature of such observation" which you say is not clear to you. What witnessing does is to be disassociated from the ego while recognizing its validity as the operational element in the body-mind mechanism which must persist as a part of the psychic construct of the psychosomatic mechanism. Such an *operational element* must obviously continue to exist so long as the body continues to exist, but it is no longer confused with the *functional essence* in the body which is common to all sentient beings -- the impersonal Consciousness.

What, quite simply, the understanding brings about is the recognition that the ego, or the mind, is merely the working partner in the physical organization that the body is, and not its independent owner as was earlier firmly believed!

As a matter of fact, it is symptomatic of your present spiritual state (certainly enviable from the relative point of view, but meaningless otherwise) that you have intuitively realized what I have said in so many words, when you say, "I could not see how someone could engage in an activity without concern for its outcome. Yesterday, I saw. So, I am currently planning to go through with this project (egoic or not)...". The meaningful words in this quote are "egoic or not". Meaningful, because the ego has lost its terror, its hold! Egoic or not -- who cares?! That is the point, my very dear friend. Why bother with the ego? Let it exist in its own place, as the *working* partner. Let intuition or Consciousness get on with its own functioning. These words of mine might suddenly raise a sudden feeling of *bravo*. Why not? Just a movement in Consciousness, witnessed by Consciousness, not of any significance.

The verse from the *Bhagavad-Gita* which you have quoted -- and which you say had moved you very much when you first read it in 1979 -- "Therefore you must perform every action sacramentally, and be free from all attachment to results", had confounded you all these years, until "yesterday", for the simple reason that you had considered it from the point of view of a supposedly independent, autonomous individual. Now the words make complete sense because the understanding has been from the point of view of the impersonal Totality. Your earlier interpretation was justified because the verse says, "*You* must perform every action...". Now you have understood the verse as, "When the understanding has taken place, every action is seen as a sacrament (part of the functioning of Totality), free from attachment to results".

Your difficulty earlier was very real: "you" could not see how "someone" could engage in an activity without concern for its outcome. "Yesterday" you saw: there was not "someone" to engage in any activity -- all activity through any individual body is part of the functioning of Totality. What has happened is a transformation from individual personality into the impersonality of Totality.

I think in course of time you will find "yourself" doing things spontaneously, without being bothered by any doubts whether there is or is not any ego lurking behind those acts.

The whole purpose of *sadhana* of any kind has been very well stated by you in your letter because it happens to be from experience: the realization that *sadhana* can bring about only quantitative changes, and that it is only the "pure understanding" of What-Is (all there is is Consciousness in which appears the totality of manifestation and its *impersonal* functioning) that can bring about the qualitative change. This understanding, being of noumenal nature (and not phenomenal or intellectual) brings about the qualitative change through merely witnessing all thoughts, feelings, desires as they arise, without getting involved in them, without identifying with them. Such witnessing, because of the disassociation with the phenomenal occurrences, brings about those glorious moments of noumenality -- the I Am -- which become more intense and more frequent as the understanding becomes deeper during the gradual process of "deliverance".

It is interesting to note the series of "happenings" which bring together the *guru* and the disciple, and thereafter the relationship becomes a confirmed one. I have come across quite a few such cases, including my own as a seeker, and there cannot be any question of a coincidence or a chance in such cases. It simply had to happen.

February 27, 1988

Maharaj had obviously "sensed" the role I am supposed to play in this phenomenal *lila*, because he had once mentioned to me that there was an abysmal misconception concerning the *guru's* teaching which a disciple is expected to convey in his own turn. He mentioned this in relation to *Pointers* when I had told him about the spontaneous (*not* automatic) writing that was taking place. He had said that several books would probably "happen" in course of time, apart from *Pointers*, and that they would not be mere parroting of his own words: while the Truth must of course remain Truth at all times, the particular aspects to be delineated would vary considerably, and to that extent the "teaching" would *appear* to have undergone some change! Quite frankly it was rather an intriguing point because I could not then imagine any such wide change (apparent though it would be) in my "teaching" as compared to that of Maharaj.

The one point that seems to obsess me is that I must repeatedly stress -- again and again to the point of irritation if need be! -- that there is really no "me" to "do" anything. And this basis must never be lost sight of when reading (or listening to) any injunction, such as "Hold on to this knowledge, and meditate...," or "A true devotee abides in the knowledge 'I Am'..." etc. The whole message is contained in the impersonality of the totality of manifestation and its functioning. And, as far as the *apparent* individual is concerned, all that can happen (at the appropriate time) is a deep understanding of this impersonality which would annihilate the very roots of the "me".

The preceding two paragraphs refer to the quotes you have given from the copy of typed translation of a talk given by Maharaj in January 1980.

I see this impersonal functioning of Totality more and more frequently as days go by (which you have described in your own case so very feelingly), and one can only gape in wondrous incredulity as one comes across instance after instance.

The most recent instance is that of a young lady from New York state, for the last ten years a follower of an Indian *guru* who has a following in the U.S. She came to see me four times over a period of about three weeks beginning in late January. She said she really did not know how or why she had made this expensive trip. The first time she saw me she felt totally guilty and disloyal to her *guru*, and knew that she would never see me again: she would spend the remaining days at her *guru's ashram* and go back and write off the entire trip as a total loss! The second time she saw me, she said, it was most reluctantly, and really was annoyed with herself for being somehow pushed into it. And, finally, the transformation was total: there was no sense of guilt concerning the *guru* because the experience had to be a step that would lead her to a much higher understanding.

You say in your letter: "During the last couple of weeks or so I've been in the I Am Consciousness more frequently and more profoundly than ever before. And yet I am amazed to find that often I seem to actually elect *not* to enter the I Am because I am more attracted to something else" You will find, my dear O., that you cease to be amazed (or otherwise) at anything that happens. Whatever happens will be merely witnessed without bothering to locate the rationale in anything that happens! -- whether it be a sudden arising of energy or "the lure of sheer laziness".

It is indeed a fact that "devotees all over the world can testify to the limitless stream of guidance one receives when the *guru* becomes a part of their lives". It is also a fact that the prevailing coincidences and synchronicities exercise a certain fascination over the "one" concerned, along with a concurrent concern or uneasiness over this very fascination. As in your case, almost again concurrently, will arise the antidote to this uneasiness with the realization that there is indeed a clear disassociation with the fascination. When the understanding is deep, again as in your case (certainly after a *lot* of pain and frustration), the core of the fascination is not the sense of achievement, but a feeling of gratitude and surrender to the *guru* or Consciousness or Totality or God.

It is interesting that in the case of D., you "suspect it may be a lack of sufficient intensity in what Maharaj called "earnestness". This is precisely the point I often "flog". The understanding cannot happen unless there is intense earnestness, and earnestness cannot be "achieved", it can only happen! And until this itself is understood (again, it can only happen), there is pain and frustration. It is for this reason that the process of dis-identification could be as painful as the living in the identified condition. The reason, of course, is obvious: the continued existence of the "me" seeking material pleasure in the identified condition, and seeking the "godly" goal of enlightenment during the process of dis-identification.

It is an interesting point that you make about the difference in your attitude which took place during the retreats: the intense concentration during the first retreat and a certain amount of distraction in the second retreat. Perhaps you will remember that during the second retreat, I had suggested to you that if at any time during a talk you felt distracted enough to walk out, you could certainly do so, and I would understand. The point is that the "process" of understanding -- certainly at the intellectual level in the beginning -- must necessarily be in *duration*, and therefore liable to alternating states of concentration and distraction, elation and depression. There is another aspect to this matter, and that is the inevitable personal relationship with the *guru*. The love for the *guru* can be a hazard if treated on a personal level because it would then be a sort of crutch on which the disciple becomes so dependent that he feels helpless in the absence of the *guru*. What is more, as an extreme case, the love for the *guru* as a person could bring on an attack of jealousy or envy as violent as in the case of two lovers! In the beginning, let me hasten to add, the love for the *guru* cannot but be intensely personal, but as the understanding gets deeper, his love continues on a personal level but is based deeper down on the impersonal love for the *guru* as Consciousness. I remember how I just couldn't do enough for, give enough to, Nisargadatta Maharaj, and his gracious acceptance of whatever I did for him and gave to him -- he knew, of course, that I was sincere and that I could afford it -- used to make me feel very happy.

I have been having a stream of visitors, and it is nice to be able to guide the eager seekers, so pitifully sincere, and so vulnerable.

March 22, 1988

It seems to me that there is a vital difference between your spiritual journal that you began in November 1978, and your letters to me which started with your letter of January 7. The difference is that the earlier record was an intended "project". However good the intention -- "to serve as an instrument that would constantly bring the focus of my attention back to spiritual matters" -- the point, of course, is that there was an intention, the futility of which was realized and the recording was stopped in September 1985.

What has happened this time is that there has been no specific intention and no "project". Indeed, in answer to my letter to you which I wrote on returning to India in December, you say in your letter of January 7: "As I start to write this letter I find I don't know what to say to you". What could possibly be anything more spontaneous (and unintentional) than that?! It is altogether irrelevant that in course of time the entire correspondence together may or may not be published, or may or may not serve any other purpose.

In any case, as you no doubt heard me say before, once the mind has turned inwards (which itself is an event over which "one" does not have any control), the process of dis-identification takes its own course, and nothing in that course can really be considered as a waste of time that could have been avoided. And so it is that you say, "the journal was not a total failure. It did bring my mind back to the subject...And from time to time reviewing it did result in what seemed to be important insights". And, of course, the journal-keeping stopped when it had served its purpose in the process of dis-identification.

There is one rather important point that I have noticed in this correspondence. It is that more and more disassociation is taking place from all that is happening to you; events are being seen as events, of course, but more importantly, reactions to the events, as and when they occur, are also being merely witnessed (which means disassociation). In other words, "you" are not afraid of the ego any longer. The ego has lost its terror because the "you" has become the witnessing. There is no longer the distressing problem of *how* to "let go". The letting-go is happening by itself, smoothly, spontaneously, naturally. You have started "floating" through life, without being particularly aware of the fact.

This leads to another interesting situation which might cause a certain amount of doubt, if not confusion. You have reached a stage (more accurately, a stage has been reached in the process of dis-identification) where the direct and constant guidance from the *guru* seems less and less necessary. And this fact could raise some feeling of unease, of disloyalty, even of guilt. What actually happens, however, is something which the *guru* has been looking forward to! What happens is that the level of duality (from the viewpoint of the disciple), in which the disciple respects and even reveres the *guru*, gives place to one of equality. This is really obvious in the sense that the *guru* has been speaking and dealing with the disciple from the standpoint of the impersonal or universal Consciousness while the disciple starts from the standpoint of the personal or identified consciousness. As the process of dis-identification goes on, the distance between the two levels decreases, formality gives way to informality, reverence gives way to friendship -- while the respect and gratitude not only never disappear but become increasingly deeper. The *guru* is delighted with this "progress" because he would abhor the situation where the *guru* has become a crutch to the disciple, where the disciple would feel totally lost without the *guru* -- a situation firmly based on the phenomenal level.

I myself remember this happening between Maharaj and myself. While I continued to give monetary and every other kind of assistance that I could possibly give to Maharaj, there was a gradual growth of informality and friendship in our attitude towards each other. And

I could sense his feeling of gratification, even perhaps a kind of pride, when he accepted me on terms of absolute equality.

It is rather interesting that the gradual change in relationship between Maharaj and myself -- for the better, of course! -- is reflected in my three books: reverence in *Pointers From Nisargadatta Maharaj*[3], a certain respectful dependence in *Experience Of Immortality*[4], and a sense of equality, essentially based on deep gratitude, in *Explorations Into The Eternal*.[5]

It is certainly a fact -- to continue with your letter -- that "things happen to us so as to bring about that Understanding". Such things have no uniformity of any kind from the point of view of the interrelated concepts of the acceptable and the unacceptable. In one case, the circumstances may seem, as in your case, "acceptable", whereas in another the need may happen to be for something "unacceptable" to happen, so that the process of dis-identification may continue on its course.

The egoic trip that you mention in this regard (i.e., the ego arrogantly seeing such "signs of grace" as indicating the Universe's special concern for one of its favorite people) is purely imaginary and unreal inasmuch as it will not appear as such when the process of dis-identification is seen as the impersonal process that it is, and is not viewed from the personal angle. You are quite correct in saying that "at the early stages at least,

---

3. ibid.
4. Ramesh S. Balsekar, *Experience Of Immortality* (Bombay: Chetana, 1984)
5. ibid.

the paradox is that for the ego to disappear it must first come to understand itself". The mind-intellect must necessarily be used in the early stages to try to understand the What-Is. Then the intellect comes to realize its own limitations, and with this surrender, intellect eventually becomes merged in the intuition. The swimmer in the early stages must necessarily use his muscles in order to struggle to remain afloat, but gradually comes to the realization that such efforts are really not necessary and that it is possible to float effortlessly: the realization happens that the body has the natural ability to remain afloat in the absence of the fear of sinking.

Regarding the different levels or types of the state of awareness, what is happening in your case is that the condition of involvement is gradually disappearing as the understanding goes deeper. More and more you are having the persistent feeling: what does it matter anyway? Some thought or feeling or desire arises, and there may be some little identification with it by way of involvement. But quite quickly, I am sure, comes the heavy feeling "what does it matter anyway?" This latter feeling cuts off vertically the horizontal involvement that was about to begin. In course of time -- perhaps even already -- the arising of a thought, the possibility of involvement, and the cutting off take place almost simultaneously. This cutting off results in a kind of vacuum which is precisely the occurrence of feeling one with the present moment. This is what Ramana Maharshi called the *sahaja sthiti* -- or natural state. There is a natural movement -- smooth and spontaneous -- from this natural state (or neutral state if you prefer the term) "upwards" when some event occurs to witness; and "downwards (deeper)" when no event occurs (to take awareness upwards) for some time, and you sink in the I Am.

The fact of the matter is that once this movement from the natural state upwards or downwards (like the unconscious shifting of the gears of a car depending on the traffic that is encountered) is seen and understood as the natural functioning of Consciousness, the "me" or the ego will find itself disassociated from the entire process. In other words, doubts or questions will then seem irrelevant in the impersonality of the movement between the three states of awareness: "the head is already in the tiger's mouth, and there is no escape" (from the happening of enlightenment).

You write about "the ego's interpretation of the significance of our correspondence", and that "the collection of our letters seems to be taking on some of the characteristics of a fetish". What you do is apparently peruse the letters from time to time, and you seem concerned about "the basis of this, although the feeling is quite strong". There is no need to analyze the event, only to witness it and watch what happens. Out of this perusal of the correspondence will no doubt arise the germ of an idea about what will ultimately take some concrete shape. Let the mind be open to the suggestions that will "come from outside". You will know what to do when the idea gets concretized.

The relationship between you and me as the disciple and the *guru* will take various shapes and concepts in the mind as it intensifies gradually, stays intensified for a while, and then almost fades away from the mind. All these conceptions (including dreams) are merely to be witnessed, even with some amusement, if you will. In such witnessing -- without any analyzing -- the ego will be absent. This would apply equally to the time whenever an effort seems to be made to get into the I Am state. Any analyzing would obviously be at an intellectual level, and merely seeing this, understanding this fact, would mean witnessing, which would cut off such intellectual analyzing which is quite futile anyway.

You will see what I mean when the three-way movement begins to happen in your awareness. The master key is witnessing without trying to find out any significance to the event concerned, which in effect means disassociation from the event; not being afraid of the ego.

March 24, 1988

I am glad to see your response to my letter of February 13.

You say that, in spite of reading that letter at least five times, "still I can't seem to get myself to talk about the essential substance of it". This is precisely the response which makes me happy. Later on, you say, "of all the letters to you, this one has been, by far, the most difficult to write. Indeed, it has been quite disturbing". The fact of the matter is that if it were a conversation instead of a correspondence, the response would have been total silence; there would have been no need of any words; indeed, any words would have been not only irrelevant, but actually irreverent, because that would have been a proof that the response was merely at the intellectual level.

In this regard, there is another kind of phenomenon which could happen, following the occurrence of a sudden understanding. It is that a peculiar lethargy or apathy could take place, a certain lack of desire or energy to do even any routine chore. There is nothing to be done about it, except, of course, to witness it, note the presence of it and wait until it disappears on its own. It might well be followed -- there is no hard and fast rule, of course -- by a sudden burst of enthusiasm, energy and inspiration, a deep feeling of joy and well being, of fulfillment, of a deep desire to do something for the *guru*, that is quite beyond the ordinary and overwhelming by any standards: the range of such feelings is quite wide. Here again, all that can be done is to take note of its presence, and "await developments".

Your reaction has not been easy for you to put down in words. It cannot be easy -- indeed, there is really no need to do so. And yet, you have said it all when you said, "...I really cannot comprehend what is going on".

Running away from the ego, and the fear of the ego both are aspects of the same concept. I am happy to note that you have recently become aware that there is a growing acceptance of the ego. You add, "But I really didn't appreciate its significance until I read your letter. Only after that did I see that this indeed did represent a diminution of any fear of the ego. I don't think I realized until just now that the underlying fear I've carried around all my life was basically the fear of the ego. (This sounds good now. Is it so?)". This is indeed good, very good. These sudden pieces of understanding happen unexpectedly, and hit like a bomb because they have a different dimension from any known to the intellect.

Your attempts at repressing the ego were actually a running away from the ego which not only exacerbated the obsession with the ego, but actually gave body to the conceptual ego. You will perhaps now recollect that this is precisely what I had been trying to convey to you ever since we met at the desert and began to have personal talks. But the bomb had to explode at the precise allotted moment! The intellect was brushing off all attempts to pierce its armor. Indeed the intellect is itself the armor which the ego wears to ward off all such attempts. Perhaps it is for this reason -- the impredictability of the hit -- that both the written word and the spoken word become necessary to bring about a situation in which the intellect at a precise moment surrenders itself, and the ego stands naked and vulnerable, exposed as the mere concept that it is.

On reading this, if there arises a feeling of joy or fulfillment or gratitude, enjoy it by all means without any sense of guilt. Maharaj must have known for some time that in my case the awakening had happened. I, of course, knew it too, but felt no need to refer to the happening so far as Maharaj was concerned. One day, however, at the end of the talk in the morning, when Maharaj was relaxing with his paan and eating tobacco (this was before it was realized that Maharaj had cancer and was subsequently forced to give it up), he suddenly looked at me and said, "I am happy that I have been instrumental in bringing about awakening at least in one case". I was overwhelmed, and I fell at his feet. Although I knew that no certificate from my *guru* was necessary, nevertheless when it did come about, suddenly and spontaneously, there was pure joy.

You say, further in your letter, that you don't really feel yet that your running away has ceased, although it has certainly slowed down. You have intuitively connected this "running away from the ego" with the concept of "witnessing", which is not of the mind but of the impersonal noumenal. You also say that you cannot really accept that you have arrived at the point where the running away has ceased. My very dear O., you need have no doubts on this point. You are like a prisoner, who has been suddenly freed from his prison, the gate is open for him, and yet having been incarcerated for a long time, cannot really accept that he is free. And the joke is -- a horrible joke -- that he was certainly behind bars, and thought he was imprisoned, but the gate was never closed and never locked. When the fact is pointed out to him, it takes him some time to believe it.

You have the key when you said, "indeed the words 'egoic or not' are becoming increasingly operational". Pretty soon, the words themselves (which are only vocalized thoughts) will not occur in the sense that any event (including a thought) will be accepted without any judgement -- and, quite importantly, even if a judgement or reaction did occur, no importance would be given to it. In other words, the events will be "allowed" to occur without bothering about any allied aspects or consequences. Some thought arises, some action takes place. Egoic? Who cares?!

I am perhaps anticipating a further development, but never mind. When this attitude of "who cares?" continues for a time, you will have reached the final veil in the form of a doubt: when I was wholly and deeply involved in material and mundane matters, I didn't care about any "ego" because I was quite ignorant about the ego, except for a general criterion of right and wrong, based on certain moral and legal rules of conduct; then my mind turned inward and I was "educated" about the ego and the need to get rid of the ego; I had thereafter been greatly concerned about the ego. And now, suddenly, I am no longer concerned with the ego: what has happened to the spiritual progress "I" thought I was making? Have I suddenly slipped back to the starting point, down the back of a snake after going up the ladder and reaching a certain point with great effort? As I have said, I am certainly anticipating this final veil -- note the 'veil" and not any real "obstruction"! When the very thought of the ego is absent, what has happened is that the deep understanding has taken over since the transformation took place from individual personality into the impersonality of Totality. The "me" is dead. Thoughts will not suddenly disappear, but when they arise, they will be "witnessed", and there would be no "one" to witness them. In fact the "witnessing" itself is a concept and therefore there cannot be any awareness of such witnessing. Who cares if there is any such awareness or not?!

You have said, "When I consider the working of the ego, I seem to be doing it with the ego". That, my very dear O., is precisely the point: why bother to consider the workings of the ego? Remember, you have stopped running away from the ego. *You are* always *in the I Am*, whether in deep sleep or awake. *The circle is complete:* the conceptual ego was never there in the first place, then it happened to get integrated, and now it has disintegrated. Who is there to bother with what? Enjoy yourself, as the sense of presence, as long as it lasts.

April 25, 1988

The strictly spontaneous "Love" feeling that came over you just before we hung up at the last telephone talk we had on March 16, was indeed the deepest dip into I-Am-*ness* that we all are, the *total* disappearance -- momentary though it might have been -- of the individual "me" which has superimposed itself on this fundamental primal state of Consciousness, which is indeed Love or Compassion, the sudden realization of which brings tears to one's eyes. This is a "dip" deeper into the love relationship between the *guru* and the disciple which is a prevailing condition *in phenomenality*, a dip into the solution of continuity between phenomenality and noumenality. Noumenality and phenomenality are not two: phenomenality is the objective expression of noumenality, and occasional dips into noumenality happen all the time. Such dips are always in the present moment, experiences of the Immortality that we really are.

You have said, "Today, for the first time, it now seems that when remembrance occurs, I am effortlessly in the I Am". You will soon come to realize that "you" are always in the I Am state. To put it more accurately, it is the I Am state which is the normal prevailing state, and the "other" state is not something alien but a normal condition in phenomenality which necessitates being "out of the I Am state". Recognizing this fact means being released from the fear of the ego.

As you know, I hesitate to give any example. But the fact of the matter is that this is something like driving along the highway in top gear -- the normal condition. Whenever you see or anticipate traffic obstruction, your foot comes off the accelerator and your hand shifts into a lower gear, until you get back into the normal top gear after the obstruction has disappeared. The "remembrance or appearance of the awareness that I was not in the I Am", that you speak of, is the awareness that, because of the anticipated obstruction of traffic, you were not in the top gear, but in the lower gear. This remembrance coincides with the disappearance of the obstruction which leaves you free to go into the top gear (of I Am) again, smoothly. To the extent that there is more traffic you will have to go into the lower gear more often and to that extent you will be less in the top gear.

Thus you will find that certain occasions (over which you really have no control) "involved a prolonged period of horrendous distraction", almost invariably followed by occasions when "I have been graced with the gift of gifts, and at long last the doubts about the I Am have gone". This shifting of gears is a perfectly natural process.

This leads to the final point of this letter, and that is your statement that "this belief that I was dependent on the Unknown for this boon (being in the I Am) occasionally engendered in me the egoic fear that this bounty might be withdrawn and I would be lost". This is the core of the matter. This fear will disappear when you remember -- or, bring your attention to the fact -- that a "you" or a "me" cannot have the bounty, that all there is is Consciousness which itself has initiated the process of identification as a separate entity. The process of identification has continued for a while, and then the mind has turned inwards and the process of dis-identification has started and gone a long way forward. All that now remains is to witness the "progress" of this process. Who witnesses this progress? Consciousness, of course. All there is, is Consciousness in which the manifestation has appeared, and in which the process of identification and dis-identification is going on as the functioning. No "me" is concerned in this process. As Ramana Maharshi has averred so positively, once the mind has turned inwards, "you" have placed your head in the tiger's mouth, and there is no escape (from the annihilation of the "me", and thus enlightenment).

April 28, 1988

The totality of manifestation is an appearance in Consciousness, like a dream. Its functioning is an *impersonal* and self-generated process in phenomenality; and the billions of sentient beings are merely the instruments (dreamed characters without any kind of volition) through which this impersonal process takes place. The clear apperception of this Truth means the irrelevance of the individual human being as a seeker, and therefore enlightenment.

All there is is Consciousness. Every event, every thought, every feeling concerning any "individual" is a movement in Consciousness, *brought about by Consciousness*. If all is water, there is no question of a drop of water seeking "waterness": -- or seeking union with water!

You say "entry into the I Am today is virtually effortless, and it remains for extended periods". Actually what happens is that the I Am is the normal state, and nowadays the movements *out of that normal state* by the mind-intellect are fewer! It only appears to you that there is an "entry into the I Am". Realization of this subtle but important fact will enable witnessing of the movements of the mind-intellect, temporarily clouding the normal state of I Am, to take place. This is merely like the temporary shifting of the gears of a car whilst driving, from the top gear to the lower gear whenever the traffic necessitates such shifting. More importantly, such realization will remove the *fear* of the ego inasmuch as the ego or the identification with the body is necessary for acts to take place through the body -- even if that body happens to be that of a *jnani*. In other words, whether it was Maharaj or Ramana Maharshi, the identification with the body had to continue so long as the body was alive, but such identification did not involve the sense of a separate do-er. Whether it was Maharaj or Ramana Maharshi, there was response when called, but the body-mind mechanism was seen as an object precisely like any other object in the manifestation.

Your quotation from *I Am That*[6] ("All these sufferings are man-made and it is within man's power to put an end to them") is most interesting as an example of the limitation of a) the language, b) the translation, c) the grasp of the visitor to pursue the point. Quite frankly, Maharaj did not have -- as he himself admitted quite often and quite openly -- the physical stamina and the patience to explain any point in detail. Also, I know he sometimes deliberately withheld a detailed explanation because he did not like to spoon-feed a disciple. (I remember an occasion when I translated something cryptic which Maharaj had said, in a very precise manner. A lady visitor, who used to attend regularly, wanted an explanation and she looked at me questioningly. Almost as a reflex, I opened my mouth to explain, when Maharaj almost shouted, "No". He wanted the lady -- who had a doctorate in Indian Philosophy! -- to figure it out for herself.

---

6. Sri Nisargadatta Maharaj, *I Am That* (Bombay: Chetana, 1973)

If the visitor concerned had pursued the point (How could the sufferings be man made when man does not exist except only as an object, a small part of the total manifestation -- and how can it be within man's power to put an end to them?), he probably would have received an appreciative look from Maharaj, and Maharaj might perhaps have explained that the sufferings were man-made in the sense that they exist only because the mind-intellect identifies itself with those sufferings, and that it is within man's power to put an end to them in the sense that when the apperception occurs that all pleasures and miseries are merely temporary movements in Consciousness, there arises a sense of disassociation from the sufferings which puts an end to them. The more subtle point, of course, is that the arising of the sufferings through identification and the end of the sufferings through dis-identification are both parts of the impersonal functioning of Totality; and that therefore the illusion of identification and the removal of that illusion through understanding and apperception cannot be in the hands of any individual who is himself an illusion without any volition of any kind.

The question then arises: What then is to be done? This can only be answered by a counter question: to be done by whom?! All there is is Consciousness, and the "human being" is merely one object in the inconceivably fantastic manifestation, and its impersonal self-generated functioning. If there is only the impersonal manifestation and its self-generated functioning, the one simple fact that stands out is that the human being as a separate entity is merely a concept, an illusion. And a mere concept or illusion cannot possibly have any duty or responsibility, any guilt or remorse to suffer from -- precisely like the character in a personal dream whose antics can only be witnessed and can never be interfered with. Such an acceptance is tantamount to a tremendous sense of freedom or relief, which is often described erroneously (giving rise to a lot of misconception) as Bliss or Love. But, whichever way it is described or labeled (quite unnecessarily), the supreme Truth is that it is not an object to be achieved by the illusory human being by any kind of illusory effort.

May 2, 1988

H. had arranged a twelve-day spiritual retreat-cum-holiday for a German group of about 32 people at a holiday resort almost at the southern tip of India.

The group was typically German: intense, deeply interested in the subject, with their homework well prepared. The reaction in the beginning was, of course, strong resistance to what I had to say. And I didn't help matters by spontaneously coming out at the very first talk that I would welcome resistance, but that, while I was quite aware of the German character (which in general I greatly admire), it was not my intention to cater to what the group might want and expect from me. All I asked for was that they give their open and full attention to what I had to say -- and then let the chips fall where they may!

It was rather interesting that on the very first day, a young man (around 30 years of age) came out with the statement that he did not have the feeling that he was in the presence of Truth, and that he doubted that "I" was an "enlightened being". I couldn't help laughing aloud. I told him that I was sorry that he was disappointed, but since I didn't expect that H. would let him have his money back, he might as well relax and listen to what I had to say. Perhaps soon, I said, he might have a clearer idea of what "he" is, what "I" am, and what Truth is. On the third day, something I said touched him so deeply that he put up his hand to ask a question. When I looked at him and smiled, he suddenly broke out into violent, uncontrollable sobbing which clearly affected several others.

All in all, it was on the whole a most interesting experience of one homogeneous group listening to a series of talks. There were at least seven or eight "transformations" of some sort -- one or two very deep indeed -- which provided the answer to why I happened to be at that place at that time.

The basis of the ultimate understanding is precisely this: that the mind turns inward not because of the initiative or the efforts of any individual but purely as a movement in Consciousness, an impersonal happening that gets misinterpreted as a personal event which is supposed to lead to some personal achievement that is labelled "enlightenment" at the higher mystical level, or at least as "peace of mind" at the more mundane level!

A gentleman called L. came to see me a few days ago by previous appointment. He was an American -- slim, gaunt of face, with a shaven head, and deep piercing eyes. He said he had been travelling for more than two years, for the last eight months in India, in search of Truth, that he had heard so much about India but that he was thoroughly disappointed: in India he had seen nothing but poverty and squalor, corruption and greed even in temples, mere parroting of the scriptures in *ashrams*, most of which were money-making rackets. He was particularly disappointed that he had not met anyone who had impressed him in any way in spite of the robes and the roles some of them had assumed. It seems he had been to the Ramana *ashram* a few days ago, and had there met a person who was reading *I Am That*. When he heard what L. had to say about his travels and travails, this person told him about Nisargadatta Maharaj and *I Am That*, and added that Maharaj was dead but he could go to Bombay and meet with me, and had also provided him with my address. I do not know who this person was.

L. said he had retired as an engineer some years ago and that he had since been a "seeker". At 55 years of age and with no responsibilities or liabilities in life, he can travel to his heart's content. He added that he had done a considerable amount of reading of scriptures of many religions, and was most attracted by the non-duality of Vedanta. It was quite obvious that the man was extremely sincere and earnest, but equally obvious that he had been misguided (although, of course, his "journey along the path" was part of the destiny of that body-mind mechanism, part of the process of disidentification that was going on).

He talked to me continuously for perhaps twenty minutes, detailing all that he had done and was presently doing. I asked him when he stopped talking suddenly (perhaps realizing that I had not uttered a word while he talked), "If you know what you are doing, where you are going, and what you are aiming at, what is your problem?" The question stunned him. He replied slowly, "Now that you put it that way, I think the answer is 'I do not know' to the question". I asked him a second question, "You have detailed the sadhana and the efforts you have put in, in order to get at the Truth as a 'seeker'. How can you seek something of which you are not aware?" He thought for a while, and again replied, "I don't know". I said, "One last question at the present juncture: what is it that made you become a 'seeker' when there surely are plenty of others known to you who are just not interested in the 'search'? Was it any special effort of your own that had started your search, or was it something from 'outside' which turned your mind inwards?" This question visibly startled him.

He sat for quite some time, bent over, with his head in his hands, in total silence. I waited patiently for him until he lifted his head, looked at me quizzically, and said, "I am afraid you have totally confused me with your apparently simple questions. Nobody has asked me such questions: nowhere in any scriptures have I come across such questions. I don't even understand the point of these questions". My answer was, "The point of these questions is that when you find the answer to these questions, you will have found the answer to all your problems".

He remained for quite a while with his eyes closed. When he again sat up, and looked at me with a smile on his face, there was a certain kind of peace in that smile which was actually quite attractive without the tension that seemed to have been a part of that bony face with the shaven head. He said very softly that no one had ever quite put the matter in that perspective. I felt an enormous sense of compassion for him. I said perhaps he had suffered enough and therefore fate had sent him here. He seemed about to make a comment; I waited, but there was no comment.

I repeated my question: what is it that had made him give up his usual mundane life and turned him into a seeker? Now he was ready to listen without arguing. So, I continued: something "outside of yourself" turned your mind inwards; you have forgotten this basic and important fact, and have since assumed the role of a privileged person -- a "seeker" -- who has done a lot of reading and put in a lot of *sadhana*, and therefore was entitled to a reward by way of enlightenment. I deliberately waited for his comment, and it came out spontaneously. "Yes", he said very quietly and very seriously, "I do expect to get enlightenment in this very body, and I am prepared to make whatever effort that is necessary".

I replied immediately and spontaneously, "You will not. You cannot". Unwittingly, and certainly unintentionally, I must have shocked him to the marrow. He perhaps took it as a curse or something because he turned white under the deep tan he had acquired during his long travels in the heat of the Indian summer. I hastened to explain, "Please understand that I do not mean that enlightenment will not happen through the instrument of the body that you call L. All I am saying is that 'you' cannot 'become enlightened', for the simple reason that enlightenment presupposes the annihilation of the 'me' as a seeker".

Thereafter we talked for almost two hours. He was on his way to a meditation *ashram*, some 100 km. away, for a period of ten days. He left saying he would come back for another talk in due course.

You have raised a most interesting point when you write, "But when I say 'exploring', I get uncomfortable since I am not 'supposed' to seek". The supposition belongs to the "me" who tries to understand the teaching that there is no "one" to seek. So, what does the me do? The me says to itself, "I am not supposed to seek; therefore I must cease to seek". And, in this ceasing to seek, the "me" continues to seek -- not positively but negatively. "Seeking" and "ceasing to seek" are both interconnected opposites of what the me is doing as a supposed entity. This seems to be an impasse. But it is an impasse only from the point of view of the me as a do-er. When the teaching -- that seeking, positive or negative, is infructuous because the apparent doer is an illusion -- is accepted *as such* (not by an individual comprehender), then the impasse disappears together with the "me". With this disappearance or surrender of the me as the seeker or the doer, a sort of euphoria descends, and whatever happens (neither seeking nor not-seeking) is merely witnessed and accepted. This euphoria is precisely the peace of mind which the me, the mind-intellect, the ego seeks but quickly resists and discards because it is unfamiliar, and it is, therefore, afraid of the state which is, in truth, our natural state: "the blessed intuitive understanding" that you speak of. But it cannot "put me out of my misery" because in that state the "me" is totally absent and does not need to be put out of any misery!

In the same context, that is to say, "seeking" which you think you are not supposed to do, you go on to say, "on the other hand, in one of his famous *sutras* Buddha makes the point that we are to believe or trust none, relying only on what our own investigations teach us". Quite frankly, my dear A., there really is no "other hand" in the Buddha's statement. What the Buddha very clearly implies is that whatever the scriptures might say, however "holy" the scriptures, nothing should be accepted with blind belief or on trust. Reliance is to be placed only on "what our own investigations teach us". These investigations are notionally divided into (in Vedanta) three stages: a) hearing from the Master's words (or, perhaps, "reading" in modern context); b) meditating thereon (and getting the doubts cleared); c) and then stabilizing in "what our own investigations teach us". Invariably, if the time and place is "ripe" and appropriate, the investigations will lead to the surrender of the investigator into the teaching of impersonality, the "no-mind" state (which would naturally include the no-intellect condition) in which the "teaching" will have been apperceived without the presence of the perceiver or comprehender: the entire manifestation and its functioning is an impersonal and self-generated process. If J. says, "...he has given up all 'seeking'", what he truly understands -- and means -- is that seeking has ceased. He has really got it all.

Again in the same context, you say, "of course I can say to myself, 'But there is none there to suffer' until I am blue in the face, but..." The situation here is very much identical to asking "yourself" who am I? You can ask yourself "Who am I?" until you are blue in the face, and absolutely nothing will happen so long as there is a "me" wanting to know the answer -- because the answer, whatever it is (actually, there is *no answer*), would naturally be at the intellectual level. Nor is the practice of Self-enquiry a *mantra* or a meditation practice. The crux of the Self-enquiry is in *not* expecting an answer; then what it does is to cut off the involvement of the mind-intellect in its process of conceptualizing, drawing on the memory for the past frustrations or successes and creating images of hopes and fears for the future.

"To say to yourself" that there is none there to suffer, is bound to evoke a reaction, "of course there is you yourself to suffer, you damn fool"! In Self-enquiry, Who am I? -- or -- Who is there to suffer? -- or -- Who wants to know? -- or..., the basis is not for the "me" to ask the question and expect to get an answer, but to *feel* the absence of any entity, any phenomenal entity which

depends for its very existence on sentience or Consciousness, and thus has no independent existence of its own. Admittedly, in the beginning it is the "me", the mind which asks the question (and expects an answer); but if the underlying principle -- the cutting off of conceptualizing -- is not forgotten, the earlier mental activity which takes the form of a thought or a feeling or a perception or a desire, or whatever, gradually gives way to a *subjective* feeling of "I", totally disassociated from the earlier identified thought or perception: the identified thought gives way to the no-mind state (at least temporarily in the beginning) without any conceptualizing. Such intermittent subjective experiences gradually lead to an effortless awareness of the *subjective* "I", the real doer, wherein the individual doing goes further and further into the background. And along with this "me" goes into the background the suffering that was associated with the "me".

May 25, 1988

Today I am 71 though I must say I do not feel the age (in the sense one would expect to feel 71!). Anyway, it is really so irrelevant from an individual point of view. Indeed, one of the Marathi Saint-poets sings in a *bhajan*, "What matters it whether this body exists or not?"

Basically, the whole point is that the problem for the individual seeker arises because he seeks intemporality within the framework of duration or temporality: he seeks the permanence of unicity in the duality of the illusory phenomenality. And then, suddenly one day -- one moment -- there is the realization that the eternal, unchanging, supreme subjectivity -- the Reality -- cannot be grasped as an object in phenomenality. And that realization is a quantum jump out of the mire of phenomenality. And this realization, when it does come about, comports the feeling "it really didn't matter -- what was all the fuss about?!" Indeed, then, you are suddenly transported back to infancy when "bondage" and "enlightenment" were unknown terms, quite irrelevant, quite unnecessary. Of course, "infancy" means innocence coupled with ignorance, whereas Realization means innocence coupled with knowledge. And even this difference disappears with the ultimate understanding that "difference" itself is only a concept in phenomenality, that ignorance and knowledge are also interdependent aspects of another concept!

When you mentioned the word "oscillations" during our talk (in connection with the understanding which on occasions seems so extraordinarily clear, and then the clarity disappears at other times), what went through my mind at that moment was the thought that these oscillations will suddenly one day "lock in" with the rhythm and harmony of Totality (not unlike the phenomenon of two oscillators which, when they are in the same field and are nearly synchronous in their pulsing, will tend to "lock in" in a process known as "mutual phase-locking" or "entrainment", with the result that they become completely synchronous). And then, what will happen, my dear O., is not so much sudden stopping of these oscillations at all, as a sudden realization that the oscillations are irrelevant, that they do not matter at all, that they only had a nuisance value to the phenomenal object *only because he was paying attention to them*, -- indeed that the oscillations must continue to occur (at least to some extent) because of the very nature of phenomenality. Waves must happen but they are of no concern to the ocean. As Maharaj used to say whenever he was asked if any thoughts occurred in his mind, "Thoughts occur, feelings occur, even desires may occur, but no attention is paid to them, and they disappear as quickly as they appeared".

I am glad you liked the report of the retreat of the German group.

There was one particular lady -- the wife of the man who actively helped H. to get the group together, called N. -- who, I think, got the little push she needed. During the personal interview, E., normally a very quiet person, suddenly started talking, at a certain stage, with such conviction and feeling that I knew she had responded to the unseen push. Words came out like a torrent, and her husband was aghast when she spontaneously remarked that she hadn't ever realized how simple the whole matter was, that there really is no chase or goal to be achieved, and finally that she would willingly give whatever she had at that moment received from me to someone who wanted it desperately (obviously meaning her husband who was then sitting by her side) but that there really was nothing to give and no one to give it to! The husband just looked at me with tears in his eyes, as E. suddenly lowered her chin and sat silent.

At the talk the next morning, someone brought up the point about the understanding being so illusive, and E. suddenly came out with the answer, "What does it matter? Nothing matters!" Everyone was astonished at the totally unexpected answer from a totally unexpected source, and the beauty of the incident was that instead of being embarrassed (as I expect the others thought), she gave me a bright smile, closed her eyes and sat silent, as her husband quietly slipped her hand between his own.

And, additionally, E.'s spontaneous remarks had a peculiarly electric effect because, as a result of participating in some therapy session some time ago when she had to scream every morning for several days, she had suddenly lost her voice, and recovered it after a time only as a sort of whisper -- and her remarks had come as a kind of exaggerated hoarse whisper in a burst of energy. My own reaction was to point a finger with my arm extended and say, "Precisely so, my dear E." when there is realization that all there is is Consciousness, let the "me" in its death throes create all the movement therein that it wants. What does it really matter? There is the deep understanding that there is really no "me" (or "you") to find any reality as some object other than itself, and that therefore what the seeker seeks cannot be anything other than the seeker himself; Consciousness will drop off its identification and find its own universality. During this process of dis-identification, let there be movements and oscillations in mind -- why bother and *thereby* keep the "me" alive?! Indeed, the apperceiving itself is the Reality (because there is no one to perceive anything anymore) which witnesses the oscillations in the mind.

Now to your letter of May 8. I was touched by your concern that I should not overtax myself on your account. There really is no choice, my dear O. Everything happens so spontaneously. Actually, after I started this letter, I received a letter from N. (yes, the same N.!) saying that several members of the group had unsuccessfully tried to get hold of the "Eleven Verses To Sri Arunachala" to which I had referred in one of the later talks at the retreat, and would I please send him a copy so that he could have copes made for each member of the group? So, I stopped this letter at the end of page 2, copied out the eleven verses from *The Collected Works Of Ramana Maharshi*[7], and sent them out with a letter to N.

The subject/object relationships in this world, in this life, are all pretty well laid out, in the sense that each supposed individual would attract a particular amount of affective benefits from the other individuals he would come in contact with as relatives or friends; also the amount of benefits he would give to others. What I mean is that all interconnected relationships -- with their relevant joys and miseries -- are clearly "stamped" at the time of the conception of each supposed individual. It is therefore quite futile to think of anyone as one's benefactor or enemy, although, of course, there is no need to deliberately flout the reasonable social

---

7. *The Collected Works Of Ramana Maharshi*, ed. Arthur Osborne (London: Rider and Company, 1972)

conventions because of this understanding. Needless to say, this applies even more significantly to spiritual relationships and their relevant material aspects. You, W., X., Y., Z., and others are examples where I am concerned; all part of the functioning of Totality.

Once the situation is understood in its very essence, it doesn't matter anymore; the show goes on and it is witnessed. There are gestures of love from some, and to maintain the balance there have been others whose nature was not to give but to take. That is O.K. too. Whatever happens is merely to be witnessed and to be marvelled at, perhaps, at the variety in the events!

My relationship with the first *guru*, which stretched itself over a period of twenty-odd years was a very peculiar one. I went to him with great hopes, but almost at once it was clear to me that what he offered me was not what I was seeking. Anyway, I continued the relationship on a tenuous basis, all the time wondering, in the early years, why I was wasting my time. It became clearer in course of time that I was to be the instrument to help him clear a relatively enormous debt into which he had allowed himself to be entangled. On my part, I suppose I was all the time getting to know the difference between the real and the superficial -- seeing the false as false. And I knew after I had met Maharaj that the twenty-odd years were *not* wasted. Later on, of course, it became clear that the question of any wastage is itself irrelevant as the illusory individual just cannot have the volition or choice which could prevent the destined event from happening.

I am very happy to read in your letter that my letters to you are gradually losing their function as a crutch, and that our correspondence is assuming its legitimate function of "maintaining a tangible link" between the *guru* and the disciple, rather than keeping a track of the progress.

I am even more delighted to read in your letter, "Thus I am not a 'me' but rather am 'seeing' or 'functioning' in general. A tree is not a thing but a process. I can readily accept this. I can actually see it". This is wonderful. Let the feeling grow. Never mind that "it has not been realized". Who is saying this? -- that it has not been realized? Who is there to realize it? The thought, however, has arisen. Fine. Just witness it. Let there not by any conscious waiting for the realization -- it would only be a "me" who would be waiting. You are already aware of this, because you at once add "And there is no frustration".

Now I can say it with confidence that it will not fatten the ego: It cannot be long now! Simply because there is no one to care how long it does take! *What does it matter?!* -- to whom?

June 9, 1988

I am glad you liked the letter to A., who shows me the sincerity of a man who knew instinctively that there is something enormously more fundamental which is the ground, the field, for everything that happens in phenomenality. I think he is beginning to realize that that is something transcending phenomenality so completely that even thinking about it -- let alone "seeking" it -- becomes a joke; that it is only when something makes one utterly "poor" (as I think Meister Eckhart used the word) and so "humble" that the "one" disappears altogether, that phenomenality (and, of course, its functioning) itself disappears like a dream on waking up.

I do really feel that cases of enlightenment would henceforth necessarily happen more and more frequently through body-mind mechanisms which are functioning as physicists and psychologists, particularly in the West. More and more, I feel, such people are opening out their minds to the fact that what they have been doing is merely scratching the surface and not going deep enough in an entirely different direction, in an entirely different perspective. I was touched when I read your words, "when I was writing scientific and technological papers I wouldn't have written what I thought was silly. Well, I now see as silly a lot of what I wrote in those 'important papers'."

And I was even more moved when I read, "And, ultimately, of course, from another perspective (or is it the same one) I am writing this 'silliness' to you at this very micro-second because that is precisely the inevitable functioning that is to take place at this moment in Totality". In such understanding -- who cares at what "level" it is! -- how can the "me" survive? And if the "me" is indeed hiding somewhere, who is afraid of it?! So long as the "me" knows who the master is (the

Functioning Element or Sentience or Consciousness), let the "me" *operate* the body-mind mechanism in phenomenality under the intuitive instruction of noumenality.

It is really a mystery how a single thought gives rise to a series of events which have a series of repercussions on a number of people. It happens to be a "mystery", however, because as Neils Bohr said to Albert Einstein, God is not really playing dice with the universe but it only seems so to us because we do not have the full information which God has. Repeatedly, therefore, I find I have to say that all is part of the functioning of Totality, and all "one" can do is to witness whatever is happening. Actually, when this is truly understood, it is also simultaneously realized that there is no "one" to witness, that witnessing takes place by itself, and that if there is a feeling of some "one" witnessing, it will almost certainly mean a personal "observing" accompanied, however surreptitiously, by comparing and judging, however unconscious.

Also, an interesting feature of the "witnessing" is the fact that events have a persistent impression of the unreality of a dream, and the witnessing is accompanied by a sense of wondrous mystery of the interconnectedness of events, but -- and this is important -- there is absolutely no desire to explore this mystery. In other words, there is then the actual experience of "Thy will be done".

As you say, in regard to the thought that occurred to you to make an assemblage of the correspondence, "What this seems to have done is to have started me to think more of you, i.e., to have you in my mind more frequently, in the manner in which the scriptures say that a disciple should keep his *guru* always in his mind".

Apart from the fact that Nisargadatta Maharaj referred as little as possible to scriptures, I have always had, ever since I can remember, a sort of distrust about scriptures because scriptures have been susceptible to various interpretations, some directly opposed to others. Indeed it was this non-dependence on scriptures which particularly attracted me to Maharaj's teaching. I had felt in my very bones, ever since I was a child, that there must necessarily be some Truth quite distinct and apart from scriptures which belonged to an organized religion and therefore necessarily differed from one another. To expect a disciple to keep his *guru* in mind all the time would naturally raise all kinds of queries and difficulties. Thus, for instance, how is it possible to keep the *guru* in mind when one is engaged in one's daily routine duties?! More important, of course, is the matter of volition: is it possible for the disciple *volitionally* to keep his mind always on his *guru*? Indeed, the very nature of the mind being movement, would not any effort to control the mind itself lead to frustration and thereby to the strengthening of the ego?! Actually, the point made in the scriptures is that events will occur in such a manner at the appropriate time that they will naturally *remind* the disciple about the *guru*. Indeed, if the disciple remembers his *guru* at odd times for one reason or another, there will be a *feeling* that he has been keeping his *guru* always in his mind. Indeed the keeping his *guru* always in his mind has no value if it has to be done consciously. It must happen naturally -- and it does when some event suddenly for some reason reminds you of your *guru* -- or you happen to be engaged in a project which concerns your *guru*. So much for the scriptures! Scriptures depend on intellect for the interpretation of the meaning. Truth is based on nothing that needs any interpretation and thus transcends meaning.

It is in a way amusing to read "I really have nothing to say to you", and then get an interesting letter from you. Perhaps you remember an older man (around 75), K., at the Desert Center. The very first day he attended the talk in the morning, he listened very attentively to what was being said. In the afternoon, he sat in the front, and said he had only one question to ask. He began by saying, "We are the dreamers of this living dream..." I did an unusual thing in as much as I interrupted his sentence with a sentence of my own. I said, "We are not the dreamers; what we are, as individuals, is the dreamed characters". I thought he would proceed with his question, but suddenly he closed his eyes, bent forward just a little, and sat absolutely silent. Before I could decide whether he felt himself snubbed, and if so, that I should explain myself, someone said something and I forgot all about K. When my attention was again drawn to him, he was looking at me with his eyes adoring, and a very gratified expression on his face.

K. wrote to me a few weeks ago, and started the letter with almost the same words, that he really had nothing particular to say to me, then went on to write a most interesting letter. He is an extraordinarily well-read man but wears his learning with grace and humility.

So, you see, I didn't have anything to say to you either when I started this letter -- and I really don't know when and where and how it will end! And that, my dear O., is precisely the point: if there is something to be conveyed it is, at the intellectual or mind level, relative; you start a letter with nothing to say, and whatever is said becomes intuitive, noumenal!

There is a small photograph of Ramana Maharshi -- perhaps the most famous and best-liked one, looking directly into the camera with the most benevolent smile one can imagine -- pasted on the wall in front of my desk. When I finished the previous paragraph, I happened to look up from my desk, right into the eyes of Ramana Maharshi, and he seemed to say, "How true!". Consciousness speaking to Consciousness, confirmed by Consciousness. All there is is Consciousness. Where is the big bad "me" to be afraid of?!

About the two questions that you ask: a) sexual distractions -- who is distracted?! Remember Yang-Chu: "Let the ear hear what it longs to hear, the eye see what it longs to see, the nose smell what it likes to smell, the mouth speak what it wants to speak, let the body have every comfort that it craves, let the mind do as it will..." Why associate yourself, why identify with the body at all? Sometimes it may be that you are less hungry than at other times. Why think in terms of "you" being less hungry or more hungry -- why not there is less hunger or more hunger? Then, when there is dis-association or disidentification with whatever happens to the body-mind mechanism -- including a greater or lesser tendency towards sex -- the prevailing tendencies of the body mind are merely witnessed *without any comparing or judging*. In such witnessing, the fact that certain changes are taking place is witnessed, without even relating such changes to "my" body. This is the point: to whichever body such changes may relate, the basic point is that it is the body to which the changes relate.

This same perspective may be carried over to your other point: b) "In times of ill health, I occasionally wonder if what was started when the head went into the tigers mouth will be allocated sufficient time to arrive at its ultimate conclusion in this particular body-mind apparatus". My very dear O., *Does it matter*? It can matter only to an entity who is desirous of such a consummation, and the entity is itself the ultimate barrier to the happening of the event called enlightenment or awakening. The entity is inherent in any desire (or expectation) whether the desire is for a lowly object or for a holy achievement like liberation. Consciousness is all there is, and whatever appears or happens is merely a movement in Consciousness. So how can there ever be any "one" to want even enlightenment? Both the tiger and the head in its mouth are concepts which disappear, merge and melt in the very Understanding. It is in this sense that Nisargadatta Maharaj used to repeat all the time, "Understanding Is All". In such understanding the entity itself gets dissolved, leaving no "one" to want or expect anything.

The phenomenal conditioning of *maya* is so powerful that it needs the pounding to be done continuously by the *guru* in order to break it.

I was extremely happy to read about your retreat with your mother for a week, and much moved with your words, "My mother was very happy".

You close your letter on a very moving note: "I am loveless". This is the natural make-up of your psyche, which contains the obvious trait of what you call lovelessness. You may not be deeply sociable, but you are certainly not anti-social. You are perhaps inclined to shun society, an aspect of, say, loneliness as an integral part of the make-up of the psychosomatic mechanism. The fact of the matter, however, is that by whatever name you may call it, it is a component of the psychic part of the mechanism -- why bother with it? That other people, who cannot understand the situation, feel offended is something that is unavoidable. The more there is the wanting to change this state of affairs, the more running away there is from the What-Is, the more aware the "me" is of what it feels it lacks. It is only when the mind-heart yields to the existing situation without any fear or hope, and accepts the lacuna unconditionally, that the understanding or transformation happens. And really the joke is that the others (who used to feel unhappy) will notice the transformation, and begin to feel that you have suddenly become more "loving".

In any event, it is a fact of life that in this world, "love" is usually mistaken for something demonstrable, like manners. True love in fact is not demonstrable. Even relatively speaking, what is true love between a man and a woman? The fact of the matter is that if one finds that the other is drawn deeply towards another, true love would allow him or her to leave, without any feeling or sense of great sacrifice! True love, relatively, would mean, "You want to leave me for someone else. O.K. You may go because I love you, and I want you to have what you want", without fear or hope or a feeling of loss.

But, truly -- not relatively -- what is Love? Love is the joy of Presence, not as "me" but as I Am; Presence as such, from moment to moment, not in duration. In duration "love" becomes a personal emotion. Love cannot be either personal or impersonal; Love cannot have any boundary or barrier. Love cannot be practiced, cultivated or brought about. Love can only happen, and then it is not the puny affective love!

June 11, 1988

I posted a letter to you yesterday. The reason for starting another letter so soon is one of those curious coincidences that have been happening to me -- and no doubt to many others -- for some time past.

This has reference to the point you made in your last letter that in times of ill health you occasionally wondered if what was started when the head went into the tiger's mouth would be allocated sufficient time to arrive at its ultimate conclusion in this particular body-mind apparatus.

This morning for no apparent reason I thought I would re-read a book I had read many years ago -- *Letters From Sri Ramanasramam*[8] -- which is a collection of letter written by a lady called Nagamma, an inmate of Ramanasramam, in Telegu (one of the South Indian languages), to her brother in Madras, one Mr. D.S. Sastri, a banker whom I knew, who collected the letters, translated them into English and brought them out as a book some 15 years ago.

When I was going through this book, I came across an incident rather similar to the point you had raised which was dealt with by Ramana Maharshi. Let me reproduce the whole incident.

A newcomer to the Asramam asked Bhagavan, "Is it possible to attain *moksha* (deliverance) while still in this body?" Bhagavan said, "What is *moksha*? Who attains it? Unless there is bondage, how can there be *moksha*? Who has that bondage?" "Me", said the questioner. Bhagavan asked him, "Who really are you? How did you get the bondage? And why? If you first

---

[8]. Suri Nagamma, *Letters From Sri Ramanasramam,* trans. D.S. Sastri (Tiruvannamalai: Sri Ramanasramam, 1970) subsequently referrred to as *Letters*

know that, then we can think of attaining *moksha* while in this body". Unable to ask any further questions, he kept quiet and after a while went away.

After he left, Bhagavan looked at all the rest of us with kindness in his eyes and said, "Many people ask the same question. They want to attain *moksha* in this body. There is a *sangham* (society). Not only now, but even in olden days many people not only taught their disciples but also wrote books to the effect that there were *kaya kalpa vratas* (rejuvenation practices and methods) and such things, and that this body could be made as strong as an adamant, so as to become imperishable. After saying all that, doing ever so many things and writing about them at length, they died in course of time. When the *guru* himself who talked and preached rejuvenation passed away, what about his disciples? We do not know what will happen the next moment to a thing that we see now. Peace cannot be attained unless through Self-enquiry one realizes that one is not the body and, with *vairagya* (absence of worldly desires and passions), one ceases to care about it. *Moksha* is after all the attainment of *shanti* (perfect peace). If therefore peace cannot be attained so long as the body is identified with the Self, any attempt to keep the body forever as it is, increases the bondage instead of decreasing it. It is all an illusion".

The point, of course, is that the individual is an illusion, deliverance and bondage are illusions, and the tiger's mouth is also an illusion. This incident is number 37 in the book. Earlier, in item 22 on *moksha*, Ramana Maharshi is reported to have said, "If you renounce and give up everything, what remains is only *moksha*. What is there for others to give you? It is always there. That Is... I should give them *moksha*, they say; it is enough if *moksha*, alone is given to them. Is not that itself a desire? If you give up all the desires that you have, what remains is only *moksha*".

The translation could, of course, have been better, but it is possible to get the sense of what the Maharshi intended to convey. The active voice in a sentence, which is so much prevalent by sheer usage, gives a misleading impression in as much as it would apparently mean that an individual is supposed to do something for anything to happen, whereas the intention is merely to convey that for anything to happen there has to be an apparent cause. Thus what is truly meant is that for enlightenment to happen, desire as such must disappear, not that "you" should discard desire. This is so very important; in effect it means that the disappearance of desire is an indication, a forecast of the happening of enlightenment; it does not mean that "you" must give up desire; it is only a deep understanding of the situation in its entirety, the understanding of What-Is as Totality that the realization *occurs* that there truly and really is no individual who can "achieve" anything, let alone so important an event like enlightenment.

Until such a realization does occur, behind the search for spirituality remains the individual with the desire for "peace of mind", and behind this "peace of mind" is the desire and hope that spirituality will mean not the end of desire but the satisfaction of all desires as they arise! And the beautifully perverse fact of spirituality is that enlightenment does not occur until all desire -- even desire for enlightenment -- ceases; and when desire ceases, somehow or other, all *needs* of the supposed enlightened individual (not desires) seem to get satisfied!!

It is with reference to this understanding of the "enlightened man" that Chuang Tzu describes the "man of perfect virtue" in obvious contrast to the average man with his constant desires and search for security: "The man of perfect virtue in repose has no thoughts, in action no anxiety... He has wealth to spare but knows not whence it comes. He has food and drink more than sufficient but knows not who provides it..."

There are needs for money, either for running the house, or giving some to relatives who need it, or whatever, and from some Belgian named P. or a German named Q. or an American named R., or... comes the needed money (and more)!

In *Letters* which I have been reading just now, I came across the following in words of Ramana Maharshi:

While I was in Virupaksha Cave, I used to eat one myrobalam every night in order to help the free movement of the bowels. Once it so happened that there were none in stock. As Palaniswamy was thinking of going to the bazaar, I asked him to bring some. Before he could go, a devotee came from the village and said, "Swami, do you need some myrobalams?" I said, "Yes, give me one or two if you have them", and he placed a large bag full of them before me.... Such things used to happen often. How many could we recollect! When mother came and started to cook for us she would say an iron ladle would be very useful, and I would reply, let us wait and see. The next day or the day after, someone would bring five or six ladles of different sizes. It was the same thing with cooking utensils. Or, mother might say it would be nice if we had this or that article, and I would mutter something; and the same day or the next such articles, ten instead of one, would be received. Enough, enough of this, I felt -- who is to look after them? There were many such incidents.

I have just received the edited manuscript of *Experiencing The Teaching*[9]. It is not a big book like *Explorations*, perhaps half of it, all in the form of dialogues. I have gone through it carefully, and my feeling is that it is a good book, particularly as a summary -- and practical application -- of the teaching, repeatedly bringing into focus as it does the essence of the teaching which is spontaneity which, of course, comports the understanding that there is truly no "one" who can do anything to bring about either the understanding itself or the spontaneous application of it as the experiencing in actual life. Notionally analyzed, what the experiencing amounts to is that there is witnessing --- witnessing happens --- that living has suddenly become, *in spite of all the usual reactions to all the usual events*, like a "dry leaf in the breeze." Nothing has changed and yet everything has changed --- nothing seems to matter: there are the usual events which may produce the usual (or unusual)

---

9. Ramesh S. Balsekar, *Experiencing The Teaching* (Los Angeles: Advaita Press, 1988)

reactions, but deep down there is the unshakable conviction that it doesn't matter what the reactions were! Is this making any sense, O.? I hope it does.

Everybody is craving for peace of mind, but never bothers to find out (for the simple reason, really, that it is not yet the appropriate time for it!) what the mind is or who it is that is seeking the peace. As soon as Self-enquiry begins the all-consuming question "Who is it that wants peace," the mind itself will disappear --- and what is mind other than the "me" who is seeking? In effect, therefore, all that the Self-enquiry amounts to is the vertical cutting off of the horizontal conceptualizing of the "me" seeking "peace" --- and *thereby bringing about peace*. When the conceptualization (which is indeed the seeking itself including the seeker) ceases, what remains is what has always been --- Peace, Love, Compassion, I-Am, or whatever. The seeker, the sought and the seeking together form the covering which hides Truth, and when this covering gets removed at the appropriate time and place, the underlying ever-present Truth shines in all its glory. And then there is the *realization* that there never was anything to be achieved, that therefore, no effort could be possibly made by any "one," that all there is, and has always been, is Consciousness in phenomenality --- the impersonal sense of Presence, I-Am --- which itself disappears and merges in noumenality when the primal energy which has produced the I-Am in phenomenality expends itself and recedes back into its source.

I have come across a copy of a statement I read out to the German group at the retreat in March/April. I thought I would reproduce it for you:

WHAT IS ACCEPTANCE?

I. Acceptance as such, basically means accepting the characteristics of any given body-mind mechanism as part of the totality of phenomenal manifestation over which the concerned individual had no control. Such acceptance leads to:

a) accepting one's own limitations not as something to improve upon with one's own efforts, but leaving the improvement, if any is needed, to the natural process. Such acceptance prevents any sense of frustration in case the efforts are not very successful;

b) accepting the natural limitations of any "other" body-mind mechanism without judging (including the inability of that body-mind, at that moment, to "accept");

c) accepting, in any love/affection relationship, the prevailing relevant positive/negative or aggressive/passive roles according to the existing natural characteristics of the persons concerned in the relationship, irrespective of sex (male or female). Such acceptance of What-Is will prevent the arising of questions such as "why should it be always me who has to give in?" Indeed, such genuine acceptance or understanding will almost certainly tend to produce a smoothening in the relationship. Any exceptionally difficult relationship will, of course, resolve itself one way or another in due course.

II. Acceptance, as such, also essentially means accepting the subjectivity of God or Totality or Consciousness or *Ishwara*, together with the existence of the "me," the identification, as merely the operational element in the body-mind organism. Such acceptance leads to:

a) accepting the body-mind organism as merely the instrument through which God or Consciousness as the Subject expresses itself objectively;

b) attention being paid wholly to the work in hand, without its being spread to the periphery through worries about the results or consequences: this obviously leads to a conservation of energy that would otherwise have been wasted in the form of tension and stress;

c) a combination of tolerance and humility which becomes utterly irresistible in human relationships. When there is acceptance about one's own limitations, there arises a natural tolerance about the limitations in "others." The resulting humility is not the interconnected opposite of "pride"; we often find that the supposedly "humble" people are some of the proudest people we know, the apparent humility being the cloak of hypocrisy. The true humility is the natural consequence of the surrender of the "me" as the do-er, always in competition with the rest of the world.

III. Acceptance/understanding very often makes the relevant body-mind mechanism extremely sensitive, and to that extent the mirrored suffering or pleasure becomes more intense: the *jnani* weeps with those who weep and laughs with those who laugh, without any sense of personal embarrassment in either case.

I prepared this brief note (which was xeroxed and circulated) when I found that there was some confusion in the understanding of the word "acceptance." This was noticed in the personal interviews. Another concept about which there seemed the necessity of some clarification was that of "Self-enquiry." I therefore prepared another brief note which was also xeroxed and circulated ---

SELF-ENQUIRY

Self-enquiry must necessarily begin with the "me". It is only in those extraordinarily few cases where there is instant acceptance of the *guru*'s pronouncement that the "me" is an illusory concept (and that all the body-mind organisms are merely the instruments through which the Totality or Consciousness as the only subjective do-er functions) that there is no need of the process of Self-enquiry.

Self-enquiry must necessarily begin with the "me" and the mind-intellect. But in such an enquiry the intellect unwittingly lays a trap, conceals it with a lot of concepts, builds an elephant pit, and then falls into it itself! It is for this reason that Ramana Maharshi says --- or implies --- that intellect can only ask the question "Who (or what) am I?" Intellect, it must be at once understood, cannot provide the answer because it *does not know* --- it *cannot know*: such knowledge cannot be objective, but only a subjective experience of I Am. You cannot *know* deep sleep, you can only talk about it in the waking state!

Therefore, to ask questions such as "Who (or what) is It that lives my life?", and, "What is my relationship with It?", is to lay a trap of conceptualization into which the mind-intellect falls very quickly and reaches the depths of despair and desperation. And then arise all sorts of doubts and problems which thrive on the "experiences" which personal efforts and *sadhana* sometimes bring about. Thus, one "sees a light" or "hears a sound" while sitting in meditation! But the point is that whenever any light is seen or sound is heard or an experience is felt, there has to be some "one" who sees or hears or feels. The question therefore must arise: Who (or what) is this someone? And the mind-intellect is back into the elephant pit.

The quantum jump out of this conceptual elephant pit cannot come out of any phenomenal effort which itself has brought about this situation. It can only *happen* when the self-generated impersonal functioning of Totality is suddenly realized, in which realization the "me," the "someone," gets annihilated. And the joke --- or the tragedy --- is that such realization can only *happen* at the appropriate time which is quite beyond the control of the phenomenal seeker in the form of a body-mind mechanism. This realization is the sudden end result of the conviction, the constantly (mentally) repeated irresistible refrain "it does not matter --- nothing matters." Matter to whom? To the "me," of course, because the "me" is in the process of being annihilated, and even this annihilation does not matter! Because what exists after this annihilation of the "me" is what has always existed in phenomenality: Love, the objective expression of the absolute subject: Love Of Oneself as Unicity.

How does this Love express itself phenomenally? It is on this point that there is some misconception regarding such expression of Love (or Compassion) by Totality through body-mind organisms in which enlightenment has occurred. What really happens is that whatever the acts that take place through the concerned body-mind mechanism, the pervading understanding is that *it does not matter* to the particular body-mind mechanism in the absence of the "me." Of course, some of these acts could raise doubts in the minds of others (not "others" to the *jnani*) until understanding happens, but the *jnani* is not concerned with such reactions just as the ordinary man, on waking up, is not concerned with the actions and reactions of the characters in the dream.

In other words, the awakening brings about the depth of the ocean. It does not necessarily stop the arising of the waves and the froth.

July 5, 1988

I have received your letter of June 20/21. Before I deal with it I thought I would tell you about a Swiss gentleman who has been visiting me for the last 20 days --- every afternoon except Sunday.

I received a letter from him on 15 April, asking me if I could give him peace of mind and answers to some questions he had been seeking for quite a long time! He added that he was quite free to spend even two months or more if I would have him. Somehow his appeal found a response in my heart, and I wrote promptly to say that I was free till the middle of August, and that he was welcome to visit me as often as he wished until then.

He arrived on June 16. He left this morning.

He was/is an unusually pleasant, unassuming, almost self-effacing man of 37, soft-spoken, obviously confused --- he had gone through a tortuous course of *sadhana* in its various forms --- and not at all hopeful of a successful visit. And yet, as soon as he began talking --- he had a slight stammer --- I could see his transparent sincerity and my heart warmed toward him. I was even more enchanted when I saw him listening very attentively, asking pointed, relevant questions only when necessary --- very receptive indeed but by no means inclined to be brainwashed. And he had certainly done his homework, having gone through certain courses of *yoga* and meditation and several other things --- and firmly rejected them.

One of the first questions he asked --- very hesitantly (his stammer became worse), very respectfully --- was whether I was enlightened and therefore authorized to answer his questions and solve his problems! I told him equally frankly that we would talk about "enlightenment" and he could decide for himself whether "I" was "enlightened," but that for his purpose, he could take it that I was. There was great relief on his face, and for a minute or two, he sat back and closed his eyes, and then quietly said, "Thank you. I am grateful. It means a lot to me." At the end of a 2 1/2--3 hour talk, there was such delight in his face that it was almost amusing and enormously gratifying. Towards the end, I said something to him which I had never told anybody until then. I told him that he would not need to stay beyond two weeks. He was enormously happy to hear it, not only because of the implication of it, but, more practically, it would enable him to book his return ticket in good time.

As days went by, I was happy to note his quick "progress."

Perhaps you would be interested in some of the points that were discussed ---

"Having understood the teaching, what do I do? How do I live in the world?"

"You *do* nothing, and you *don't do nothing*. You merely let whatever happens happen without any sense of having done anything. In other words, "you" do precisely what you have been doing without the sense of any "you" doing anything. Everything that happens is merely witnessed, without any comparing and judging by any "me."

"What is my true nature?"
"Your true nature you know when you are in deep sleep."
"But I do not know anything in deep sleep."
"Quite so. You *cannot* know anything in deep sleep."
"What does that mean?"
"It simply means that your true nature is the absence of the 'me' that wants to know his true nature."

You have ten thousand photographs of yourself taken every day in different poses in different costumes. One or more photographs get destroyed. What happens? So if one person or more persons on this earth die, the bodies are of course destroyed. But what happens to That of which all bodies are multiple representations?

Nothing, of course.

You are climbing a hill and you reach the top, rest on a bench and enjoy the cool breeze: feels good! You are hungry and thirsty, so you eat some sandwiches and take a long drink out of the flask: feels good! A nagging problem that was bothering you all day disappears: feels good! The "you" feeling good is present only when the occasion is resurrected out of the memory. At the time it felt good, it just felt good --- there was no "me" feeling good. The good feeling left as soon as the "me" trespassed on the present moment, bringing with it the misery of the past and the fears of the future.

You go to sleep and you dream. You wake up and the personal dream is over, but the living dream begins. In other words, you wake up from the personal dream into the living dream. It is only in deep sleep that there is neither the personal dream nor the living dream --- because in the deep sleep state there is no separation of the "me-and-the-other." Apperception of this fact means awakening to your true nature.

When the understanding of the non-dual nature of noumenality and phenomenality is full and deep, even the *mahavakya* like "That Thou Art" becomes an unbearable abomination. The *mahavakya* was necessary for the notional understanding so long as there was a "me" as a separate entity. But unless the intellectual understanding based on the notional duality between That (as the Absolute Subject) and Thou (as the individual object) and the need of a merging between the "two" is transcended by sudden apperception, the *mahavakya* itself remains as the bondage. The ultimate understanding can only be that Consciousness is all there is --- as noumenality when at rest (unaware of itself), and as phenomenality (aware of its presence as appearance) when in movement.

It was gratifying to see M. take these statements --- and many more --- in his stride. There was often a sort of glaze which would come over his eyes, and when, only occasionally, he paraphrased my words in order to have a confirmation of his intellectual understanding, he did it so precisely that it really did not need any confirming.

My latest visitor is another M., from Canada. He came yesterday and the two M.s met for almost the entire session of four hours. They took to each other at once, and it was interesting to see the Swiss M. enthused off and on, during the discussion, to talk direct to the Canadian and explain the points according to his own understanding and experience.

I have just gone through your letter again, and it is rather interesting to note that you really do not have very much to say about the teaching, and this correspondence is turning definitely to a mere keeping in touch with each other.

I am glad you have talked yourself back into doing the booklet. Somehow I find myself quite enthusiastic about this effort of yours, perhaps because it will not be something actually written through me like the other books.

The changes in one's perspective keep on happening all the time, and just witnessing them impersonally without comparing or judging can be an instructive spontaneous spiritual exercise.

Milton Keynes UK
Ingram Content Group UK Ltd.
UKHW011313310823
427835UK00001B/27